Teenage Pregnancy and Poverty:
The Economic Realities

Teen parents are not always prepared for the many costs involved in raising a child.

The Teen Pregnancy Prevention Library

Teenage Pregnancy and Poverty:
The Economic Realities

Barbara Miller

THE ROSEN PUBLISHING GROUP, INC.

NEW YORK

Published in 1997 by The Rosen Publishing Group, Inc.
29 East 21st Street, New York, NY 10010

First Edition
Copyright © 1997 by The Rosen Publishing Group, Inc.

Manufactured in the United States of America

Library of Congress Cataloging-in-Publication Data
Miller, Barbara.
    Teenage pregnancy and poverty: the economic realities / Barbara Miller.
        p.   cm.—(Teen pregnancy prevention library)
    Includes bibliographical references and index.
    Summary: Discusses the problem of teen pregnancy and how it affects
the economic future of the persons involved.
    ISBN 0-8239-2249-9
    1. Teenage mothers—Juvenile literature.   2. Teenage pregnancy—
Juvenile literature.   3. Women—Health and hygiene—Juvenile
literature.   4. Public welfare—Juvenile literature.   [1. Teenage
mothers.   2. Pregnancy.   3. Women—Health and hygiene.   4. Public
welfare.]   I. Title.   II. Series.
HQ759.4.M55   1997
304.6'32'0835—DC21   96-40416
                                                                          CIP
                                                                          AC

Contents

Dating can be an important part of your life, but you should also be aware of the risks of sexual activity.

1 Teen Pregnancy: What's the Problem?

IN THE UNITED STATES AND IN MANY OTHER countries around the world, adolescence is supposed to be a period between childhood and adulthood when young people learn about what is expected of them but are still considered too young to handle adult responsibilities. Not really children anymore, teenagers are still "kids" who are supposed to be going to school, spending time with their friends, starting to date, and perhaps working part time to help support their families or put money away for college.

For some teenagers, however, adolescence *does* involve adult concerns. In the United States, 1 million teenage girls become pregnant every year. By the age of nineteen, one in four black women and one in seven white women are already mothers. Seven percent of young men become fathers while they are still teenagers. Nearly one quarter of teens who have a baby have a second within two years of their first. These young parents are suddenly faced with huge responsibilities and confusing choices.

Studies tell us that 85 percent of teen pregnancies are not planned. This means that the vast majority of girls who become pregnant do not know about, are afraid of, or simply don't use effective birth control methods. What happens to teens who become parents? What kind of choices do they make when faced with an unplanned pregnancy? About one third of pregnant teens have abortions, and about half keep the baby to raise themselves. Six percent put their children up for adoption. What are the consequences for the future if teens decide to have and raise their children? What kind of life is in store for a baby whose parents are teenagers? Does becoming a teen parent mean that you and your baby will be poor?

Teenage pregnancy has become a key issue in debates about sex education, making condoms available in schools, and welfare. Controversial new laws promise to change the welfare system radically. Will drastic changes in the welfare system keep teens from having babies? Is a two-parent household any guarantee against poverty? Does sex education in schools actually encourage teens to become sexually active, as some people believe? Or is sex education a necessary part of preventing teen pregnancy?

There are many assumptions about who teen parents are and what happens to them and their babies. Some assumptions are based on facts; others are falsehoods. This book will explore the myths and realities of teen parenting and will focus especially on the relation of teen parenting to poverty (being poor). It isn't always easy to figure out what is right or wrong. The following chapters address some complicated questions about the causes and consequences of teen parenthood.

2 Which Teens Are Having Babies and Why?

THE ALAN GUTTMACHER INSTITUTE REPORTED in 1994 that 56 percent of girls and 73 percent of boys under age eighteen are sexually active. The Institute also found that 60 percent of teenagers from poor families are sexually active, compared to 50 percent of teenagers from higher-income families.

Many sexually active teens use some form of birth control in order to avoid pregnancy and sexually transmitted diseases (STDs) such as AIDS. However, teenagers from low-income families are twice as likely as teens from higher-income families to have an unplanned pregnancy while using condoms or birth control pills. In other words, while poorer teens might use birth control almost as frequently as wealthier teens, they may make more mistakes and use it incorrectly.

What About Family Income?

The overwhelming majority of teenage births are a result of unintended pregnancies, meaning the teen

Teenagers who have goals for the future and a strong support system are less likely to become parents at a young age.

mother did not really mean to get pregnant. What are some of the factors that make some teens decide to have an abortion? Why do some teens decide to become parents?

Studies show that a young woman's household income has a big impact on what she decides to do after she becomes pregnant. The majority of girls who have abortions come from households that are relatively wealthy. The poorer a pregnant young woman is, the less likely she is to have an abortion.

Many poor people depend on the publicly funded Medicaid program to provide for their health care, and Medicaid does not provide funds for abortion. It is easy to see why abortion is not a realistic choice for a lot of young women. Even clinics that provide abortions at a lower cost than private hospitals charge a few hundred dollars.

Research shows that girls whose parents have had many years of education tend to put off having children longer than other girls. Girls who feel positive about their future are more likely to choose abortion than those who feel that their future is bleak. Child-bearing is most concentrated among teenagers who come from poor or low-income backgrounds. Eighty percent of the young women who give birth fall into the low-income category. Statistics show that black and Latina girls are more likely than white girls to keep their babies and become teen mothers.

Pregnancy Choices

Even though many young women decide to have abortions when they learn of their pregnancies, for many others abortion is out of the question. Usually this is because their religious beliefs prohibit abortion.

Charlene and Brendan had been dating for six months. They were both seventeen. Their religious backgrounds taught them that no one should have sex before marriage, and that abortion was a sin.

One night after a party, they went back to Charlene's house. Though they had always tried to avoid going "too far," this time they couldn't help themselves and had unprotected sex. A month later, Charlene learned she was pregnant. Though by now she realized that she and Brendan were not meant to be together, she felt she couldn't punish her unborn child for her irresponsible behavior. Charlene believed having an abortion would be an even bigger sin than having sex in the first place. She decided to have her baby.

Pregnant by Accident

Sometimes a pregnant young woman will hide her condition from friends and family out of embarrassment or shame. By the time her pregnancy is discovered by others, it can be too late to have an abortion even if she wanted one. Abortions usually take place during the first three months of pregnancy. Any later than that may be dangerous to the mother's health.

Doreen was sixteen when she started dating James, a boy she met at a party. Though she had never had sex before, she felt she wanted to let James be the first. She was concerned about using birth control, so she asked James what they should do. James said he would pull out of her before he ejaculated, promising her that this would work.

Soon after the first time they had sex, James stopped calling Doreen. She didn't see him around the neighborhood, and a friend told her he had moved away. About two months later Doreen still hadn't gotten her period. After three and a half months, she figured she was probably pregnant but didn't know who to tell or what to do. She knew her parents would be really mad at her. She thought none of her friends would be supportive, since none of them had ever had sex before, and she was too embarrassed to tell them that she had.

After five and a half months, Doreen couldn't hide her secret anymore. She finally admitted to her parents what had happened, figuring she would just have an abortion. She didn't realize that her pregnancy was so far along that an abortion would be too dangerous.

Doreen's experience demonstrates how important it is to have all the facts about birth control. "Pulling out" before ejaculation (the release of semen when a male has an orgasm) is *not* an effective birth control method. Sperm can be released before final ejaculation, even though you might not notice it happening.

This story also brings up the fact that sex and pregnancy can be hard topics to talk about with your parents, your friends, or your doctor. But it's important to get the facts. Pick an adult you trust, and ask as many questions as you can.

Talk to an adult you trust about avoiding pregnancy and sexually transmitted diseases.

Why Do Some Teens Choose to Become Parents?

What about girls who choose to become pregnant while they are teenagers? Though the majority of childbirths among teens are unplanned, a number are the result of a choice by the teen to become pregnant. About 14 percent of teens who give birth become pregnant on purpose.

In some cases, older teenagers who have decided to get married may decide to start their families early. If the marriages work, they can be the start of potentially long, stable family lives. But these cases are rare. Most teen mothers—about 71 percent—do not marry or live with the baby's father. And few teenage girls have the financial resources to raise a family on their own. In fact, the fastest-rising pregnant population is young teenage girls who have very limited financial resources.

What are some reasons that might lead a young woman to become pregnant, when she still has so much growing up to do herself? There are many answers to this question. The following are some examples of what kind of situation or state of mind might influence a girl to want to have a baby before she is emotionally or financially prepared.

Some girls talk about wanting something to call their own. Maybe they don't get the kind of love they need at home, and they think that having babies of their own might make up for this.

Jillian is fifteen years old and the middle child of five siblings. Her parents are divorced and her mom works full time to support the family, which is a constant struggle. Jillian gets kind of lost in the middle of things and doesn't get much attention from anyone in her family. She knows some kids at school who have had babies recently, and it seems like such a cool thing to do! She thinks to herself, "If I have a baby, it will always be with me, and we can love each other no matter what!"

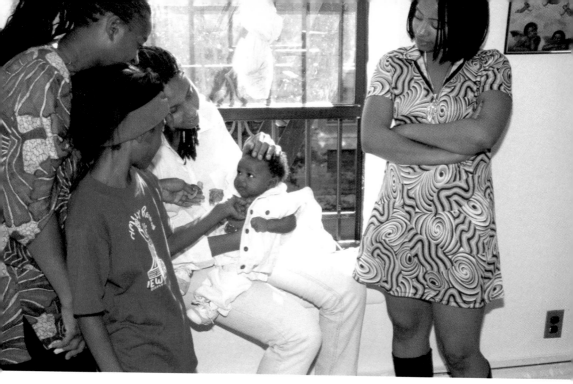

When a friend has a cute baby and receives a lot of attention, it can make you want to have a baby too.

What Jillian might not realize is that having a baby is a huge responsibility. Having a baby changes your life forever. A baby should never be thought of as simply someone who will love you. You have to be able to *give* endless amounts of love and to sacrifice a great deal for your child.

Perhaps a girl is in a hurry to grow up and thinks a baby is a sign of adulthood. Some girls may see their friends having babies and get pregnant themselves just to get the same kind of attention.

Tanya just moved to a new neighborhood and wants very much to make new friends. She just turned sixteen and all the girls in her new school seem so much more grown up than she is. She has noticed that a couple of the most popular girls in the school have babies. They always bring baby pictures with them to school and sometimes even take their babies to school with them. Everyone always makes a fuss over them and their babies. "If I had a baby," Tanya thinks, "I would probably be more popular."

Do you think having a baby is the answer to Tanya's problems? She might think it will make her life easier, but having a baby definitely *does not* make life easier. Peer pressure to be part of a popular crowd is something all teens deal with from time to time. Sometimes, as in Tanya's case, doing something just to be popular can have serious consequences that will affect the rest of your life. You probably have a pair of shoes or jeans that were once "cool" and now sit at the back of your closet. A baby is a person, and can't be put away once it's not cool anymore. Tanya will realize this when it is too late.

What About the Boyfriends?

It takes two people to create a pregnancy—and to prevent one. Negotiating issues of birth control with boyfriends is not always easy. Some young

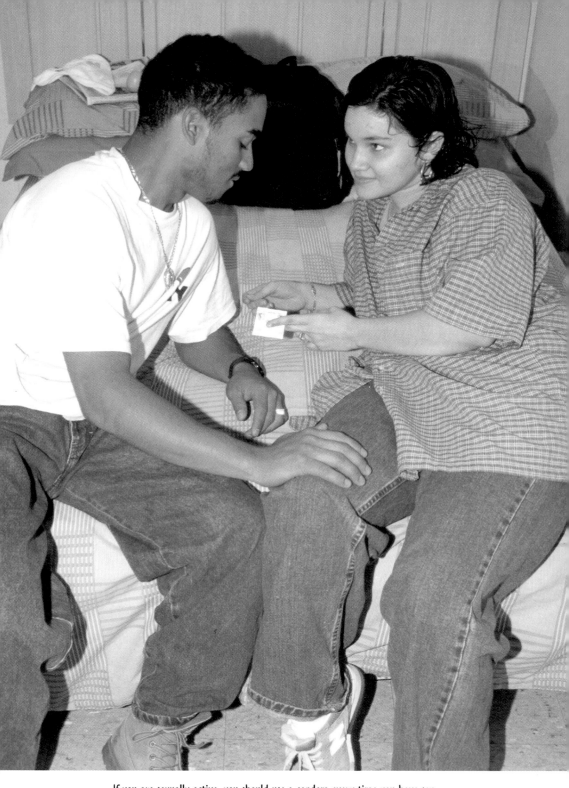

If you are sexually active, you should use a condom every time you have sex.

men are aware of the importance of using condoms, especially to protect themselves and their
partners from AIDS. But some young men try to
argue with their girlfriends about using condoms or
other forms of birth control. All too often a young
man will say something like, "If you really loved
me, you wouldn't make me wear one of those
things." Such an attitude not only increases the
danger of pregnancy, but puts both partners—and
their unborn child—at risk of contracting HIV, the
virus that causes AIDS, and other sexually transmitted diseases.

Creating a baby is seen as a status symbol for
some guys—a sign of their masculinity. A girl might
be pressured by a boyfriend to have his baby so she
can "prove" she loves him.

*Trisha and J. C. have been dating for a few months.
Trisha is a fourteen-year-old high school student, and
J. C. is a nineteen-year-old who dropped out of school
last year. Trisha wants to have sex with J. C. but has
been putting him off because he insists he won't use
condoms. Trisha knows there are pills and other things
she can use as birth control, but she's too afraid to go to
a doctor for a prescription. Meanwhile, J. C. says he
won't wait much longer for her to decide to sleep with
him. Trisha knows she could get pregnant, but she likes
J. C. and doesn't want to lose him. If she does get*

pregnant, J. C. has told her not to worry, because he wants her to have his baby. This worries Trisha, since she knows of another girl who had a baby with J. C., and he doesn't help pay for or take care of it. She reassures herself by thinking, "It'll be different with me."

Both partners must take responsibility for birth control. Both boys and girls are sometimes guilty of neglecting to use contraception. Even choosing not to be careful enough is like choosing to get pregnant.

It is easy to assume that most fathers of children born to teen mothers are teenagers them-selves. However, this is not the case. Only 26 percent of men involved in pregnancies among women under age eighteen are teenagers them-selves. Nearly one-third of the fathers of babies born to fifteen-year-old mothers are six or more years older than the girls. Alarmingly, the majority of fathers of children born to teenage mothers are over the age of twenty, and many are over the age of twenty-five. Some research indicates that a sig-nificant number of births to teenage girls are the result of rape by men who are in their twenties. This information is important because it tells us that for many teen girls, getting pregnant is not a choice they make.

Most teen pregnancies occur among couples who are not married.

Why Are More Unmarried Girls Having Babies?

The majority—about 71 percent—of teenage girls who have babies are not married. In 1980, only about 48 percent of teen births occurred outside of marriage. The percentage of first births to teenagers that occur outside of marriage has increased even more dramatically since the early 1960s, when it was only 33 percent.

Why are so many unmarried girls suddenly having babies? Some say it is because of a change in ideas about the family. With so many children being raised by single or divorced parents, teens may find it more acceptable to become single parents themselves. Another reason might be that the large numbers of young immigrants in North America are from countries where having babies at a young age is relatively common. The children of immigrants, if born on U.S. soil, are automatically citizens.

Advertising, music, television, movies, and other forms of popular media may also influence teens to have premarital sex. Sexually explicit song lyrics and images in music videos send the message that sex is fun and exciting. Television shows and movies often show people having casual sex, usually without mentioning birth control. The consequences of un-safe sex are rarely shown.

Another reason could be a lack of information in schools about abstinence and effective birth con-trol. Research shows that boys receive even less sex education in school than girls, and are less likely to talk to their parents about sex.

Supporting Roles

Many girls who have babies while they are still living at home depend on their families to support them and their children. Most of the time, teen mothers do not move in with the baby's father, and more than half of teen mothers don't receive enough money from the baby's father, even though the law requires him to pay child support. Over half of young mothers aged fifteen to seventeen still live at home. It is easy to see why having relatives around is a big help to young mothers, especially those who are still attending school. Often, a grandmother will help with child care. Some girls help their families by getting part-time jobs; some are supported by the baby's father; and some turn to the welfare system for support. Most girls rely on a combination of the above resources to care for themselves and their babies.

Life can be especially difficult for young women whose families disapprove of their pregnancies and refuse to help them. If the baby's father also refuses to help, the young mother may be completely on her own.

Is it wrong for a teenager to have a baby when she doesn't have much money? It is true that having a baby as a teenager is usually not a responsible thing to do. But there are many who feel that unmarried teen parents are morally wrong, that teen parents are responsible for rising welfare costs in the United States, and that they raise children who follow the same path. Is there any truth to this? The next chapter will look at some myths and facts about how much teen parents rely on the welfare system.

3 Teen Pregnancy and Welfare: Myths and Facts

RAISING A BABY IS VERY EXPENSIVE. BELOW IS a list of the costs involved in getting everything a baby needs in its first year.

FOOD	$950
DIAPERS	$650
CLOTHES	$475
FURNITURE	$1,000
BEDDING	$350
HEALTH CARE	$450*
TOYS	$250
DAY CARE	$2,000
TOTAL	**$6,125**

* If the baby has a medical problem, health care will probably be much more expensive.

We know that the majority of teens having babies are poor. How are they paying for the care of their children? Many people feel that American

It is very expensive to buy everything a baby needs.

taxpayers pay teen parents' bills through taxes used to support the public welfare system. Are there really so many poor teen parents on welfare? To answer this question fully, we need to understand what welfare is. The next section looks at how welfare began and how it has changed.

The Welfare System

Since 1935, public welfare has been a source of aid for single mothers and their children. Public welfare for poor mothers began as a way to help families remain together. Before there was any welfare, many single women had to place their children in orphanages because they had no way to care for them. If a woman did keep her child, she often had to work so many hours a day that the child was not supervised properly.

Welfare was created in part because many people in government felt the proper place for a woman with a child was in the home. People thought poor mothers were entitled to help from the government. Welfare helped make it possible for poor women to provide adequate care for their children.

Times have changed since then, and ideas have changed about entitlement programs (government programs that guarantee and provide benefits to a particular group of people). Most people no longer believe that poor mothers should depend on the government for money. Many people point their fingers at poor teens who have babies and see them as lazy, irresponsible kids. Others argue that teen mothers go against national values about what makes up a "good" family.

Irina saw herself as different from most of the girls she knew in her neighborhood. While most of the other girls were out chasing boys and hanging out in the nearby park, Irina sat at home and read books. Last year, Irina met Tommy in school. Like her, he was a good student and read a lot. He promised all sorts of wonderful things if she would only be "his girl." But once she was "his," he suddenly decided he didn't want anything to do with her. Irina was hurt and sad. When she learned that she was pregnant, she was scared too. But she decided that she didn't want to give up the baby that was growing inside her. She figured she'd find some way to get by. Her father had a good job. When she had her baby, her parents helped support her.

When the factory where Irina's father worked as a foreman closed down, she knew that she and her baby needed more help. She decided to finish high school at night and look for a full-time job. But getting a job without a diploma would not be easy. Until she found one, she had no other choice than to turn to welfare for help. She dreaded her visit to the welfare office, and felt embarrassed about it. The experience was even worse than she imagined. She saw people staring at her on the street as she walked into the building with the baby. One man even muttered, "Go get a job." If he only knew how hard she was looking! The caseworker at the welfare office talked to her as if she were a baby herself, telling her that she better get her life together, because the government wasn't going to make her life so easy forever. "Easy!" thought Irina. "I'm barely going to be able to feed myself and the baby on this money! I can't wait to get a job!"

AFDC and New Welfare Laws

For decades, when people talked about welfare, they were usually referring to Aid to Families with Dependent Children (AFDC). In addition to AFDC,

Some teen mothers receive money from the government to help them buy food and other necessities.

welfare also includes Social Security, home relief, food stamps, and other programs. However, AFDC has been by far the largest, most expensive program within the welfare system.

In 1996 a new set of laws was passed that completely changed the welfare system in the United States. Basically, there is no AFDC anymore. Instead of the federal government being responsible for providing money for the poor, it will provide "block grants," or big sums of money, to each state, and the state will decide how to run its own welfare program. The states have to follow certain rules. There is now a limit of five years that a family can receive welfare benefits. This is the first time there has ever been such a limit. Unmarried teen moms will generally be required to live with an adult and stay in school in order to receive benefits.

Teen Moms in the Welfare Debate

In all the debates about changing welfare laws, it is young—and usually minority—single mothers who have been the main focus. These young women, many argue, are putting the greatest strain on the welfare budget, and their children are most likely to remain dependent upon welfare for basic needs.

Many stereotypes have emerged about "welfare moms." These women, some people believe, have babies *because* they want the welfare money. Today, many people talk about welfare as a "free ride" for

Many teen moms must add a part-time job to their many responsibilities.

some mothers, which costs the government too much money, and encourages out-of-wedlock births. There are many powerful lawmakers who believe that if teenagers could not get welfare to take care of their babies, they would simply stop having them.

Others argue that there is no evidence suggesting that girls have babies simply to receive welfare money. They argue that cutting off welfare will only produce more hungry children, not reduce the number of babies born. People on this side of the debate say that we need to create better and more accessible health care for the poor, including more information about birth control options. This would help reduce pregnancy. Also, if there were better job opportunities for young women, fewer would need to depend on the welfare system.

There is so much heated debate about this topic that it is hard to know what to believe. Certainly, it is a problem that many young women who cannot support themselves are having babies.

However, are single teen moms really the major group receiving welfare? Do young women really have babies just to get welfare money? Shouldn't we also look at teen fathers, many of whom do not take responsibility for their children, leaving the teen mothers to fend for themselves? In searching for answers to the questions surrounding the controversial issue of teen pregnancy, many myths have arisen about teen mothers and the welfare system. Using recent statistics from national research centers that are trying to get to the bottom of this issue, we will look at both the myths and the facts of teen pregnancy and poverty. Some of these "myths" are not completely untrue.

MYTH: Teenage mothers are a big drain on the welfare system.

In fact, teenage mothers made up only 5 percent of the total population receiving support from AFDC. Also, out of this 5 percent, almost all of the girls were older teens, aged eighteen or nineteen, and not young teenagers. But the picture becomes more complicated when you consider that half of the total population receiving AFDC were women who gave birth while they were teens. In other words, while a teen with a baby might not go on welfare right away, statistics show that she is likely to be on welfare in the future. An estimated 53 percent of money given out through AFDC went to support families formed by a teenage pregnancy.

MYTH: Teen moms wind up trapped in a life of poverty.

Teenage mothers do face more challenges than other girls their age. But the economic differences between teen moms and their peers may not be as big as you might think. About 25 percent of adolescent mothers receive welfare by the time they reach their early twenties, compared with 19 percent of women who waited until their early twenties to give birth. As teenage mothers get older, many eventually stop needing welfare. However, even in their late twenties and early thirties, women who became mothers when they were teenagers are more likely to be on public assistance than those who first gave birth in their early twenties.

MYTH: Welfare benefits keep getting better and better.

Some believe that the government keeps raising the amount of money given to welfare recipients. This is untrue. Between 1970 and 1993, the number of families on AFDC increased 163 percent, from 2 million to about 5 million. During that same time period, the average monthly AFDC benefit per family declined 45 percent, from $676 a month to $373 a month.

MYTH: Getting married means you're less likely to be poor.

Raising a child with two parents is no guarantee against welfare or poverty. In fact, 25 percent of teenage mothers who are married when they give birth go on welfare within five years of the birth of their child.

MYTH: Girls have babies because they want welfare money.

The fact is that the overwhelming majority of girls who have babies did not plan to do so. Also, the number of teen births has risen as the amount of money paid through welfare has fallen. Welfare is an increasingly less attractive or realistic way to support a family.

Another argument against the myth that welfare encourages poor women to have babies is the fact that a number of countries with lower teen birthrates provide more generous welfare benefits to single mothers than the United States does. For example, the birthrate in the United States is sixty-two per every 1,000 females aged fifteen to nineteen. For the same age group, the birthrate per 1,000 is nine in France, ten in Italy, seventeen in Norway, twenty-two in Australia, twenty-five in Canada, and thirty-three in Britain. If welfare made women decide to have babies, then these countries would have teen birthrates similar to the rate in the United States.

MYTH: Welfare will always be there to help.
Welfare benefits to help take care of poor families with children have been available since 1935. However, the government's commitment to taking care of families in need of assistance has changed dramatically.

Under new welfare laws, poor families will no longer be guaranteed welfare benefits. In addition to the new limit of five years of welfare benefits, there are some new rules for teen mothers receiving welfare. Teen parents have to stay in school or work part time in order to get benefits. Also, unmarried minors (persons under eighteen) are now required to live with an adult, or in an adult-supervised home. Under new welfare laws, there will also be an increase in teen pregnancy prevention programs.

One of the biggest changes in the new welfare system is that legal immigrants—people who live in the United States legally but are not U.S. citizens—

are no longer eligible for welfare benefits in most cases. Many teen mothers in the United States fall into this category.

There are many reasons why changing the welfare system is important. In recent years, the number of families on AFDC rose dramatically. Even though the average monthly welfare check has declined about 45 percent during this period, the government still paid out more money than ever through AFDC. In 1991, for example, U.S. taxpayers spent over $29 billion on AFDC, Medicaid, and food stamp payments to families that started when the mother was a teenager. This figure was $10 billion higher than in 1988.

At the same time, the idea that welfare money given to poor women with children takes up a big percentage of the national budget is false. In fact, only a small fraction of the national budget is spent on welfare.

Teens do not intentionally have babies in order to collect welfare money, despite what some people think. Nor are teen mothers draining away taxpayers' money. But it is true that times are tough for teens with babies. Having a baby as a teen makes it that much harder to finish school, go to college, and get a good full-time job. It also makes it harder to stay off welfare later in life.

4 Health Facts

NICOLE GOT PREGNANT WHEN SHE WAS SIXTEEN.
For the first few months of her pregnancy, she was too embarrassed and frightened to tell anyone besides her boyfriend, Hector. He was scared, too. Neither of them knew what to do. They didn't know that Nicole should go to a doctor for prenatal care, or that she should stop eating her usual diet of chips and soda. In fact, during most of her pregnancy, Nicole was too stressed out to eat much at all.

The baby was born prematurely and needed special care all the time. The doctor said this was because Nicole hadn't gotten medical care soon after she got pregnant and because she hadn't eaten well. Nicole and Hector were worried. Even after they got the baby home, the infant didn't gain weight very quickly. Both Hector and Nicole had to quit school and get jobs to pay the medical bills and other expenses. They wanted to do what was best for their baby, but they also felt that they were too young to have to worry about a little baby's health. It was a lot of pressure.

Studies show that children born to teenage mothers are at risk of poor health. One third of pregnant teenagers receive inadequate (not good enough) prenatal care (care of the mother and baby before the baby is born). Teenagers may not seek proper medical care because of embarrassment, because they don't know that they should see a doctor, or because they can't afford it.

Not receiving medical care can be an expensive mistake if the mother develops a problem during pregnancy or if the baby is born with an illness or disability. It is very expensive to care for a child with medical problems. Few teen parents or their families can afford this expense.

Here are some health facts about teen mothers and their babies:

FACT: Teens age seventeen and under have a higher than average risk of pregnancy-related complications, including premature delivery and anemia (too few red blood cells).

FACT: The likelihood that a woman will die while giving birth is 60 percent higher for mothers under age fifteen than it is for women in their twenties.

FACT: The younger a woman is, the less likely she is to receive early prenatal care.

FACT: A lack of early prenatal care occurs among teens of all racial and ethnic groups.

AIDS, which is almost always fatal, and other diseases such as chlamydia can be caught through sexual activity.

FACT: Contrary to what other statistics indicate, wealthier pregnant teens are *less* likely to receive early prenatal care than poorer teens.

FACT: The poorer a woman is, the more likely she is to have a baby who doesn't weigh enough when it is born.

FACT: Babies of adolescent mothers are more likely to be premature, have low birthweights, and require hospital care within the first five years of life than babies born to women over twenty.

FACT: Infants who do not receive the right kind of care before they are born are forty times more likely to die as newborns than infants who do receive good prenatal care.

Whether they have babies or not, teens who are sexually active face a number of health risks, some of which are deadly. Every year, 3 million teens catch a sexually transmitted disease (STD), which can be life-threatening, or can make it difficult or impossible for them to have children later on. Some common STDs include gonorrhea, chlamydia, syphilis, and genital herpes.

Probably the most serious and deadly STD is AIDS (Acquired Immunodeficiency Syndrome). AIDS occurs after the body is infected with the Human Immunodeficiency Virus (HIV). This virus enters the body through the bloodstream or other body fluids. A common way to be infected with HIV is by having unprotected sex.

Unless a male wears a condom during intercourse, he and his partner will exchange fluids that could carry HIV. If you are sexually active, you should only have intercourse with the protection of a condom. The only way to guarantee full protection against pregnancy or the spread of STDs like AIDS is to practice abstinence (not have sex at all).

If a woman is infected with HIV, it is likely that her baby will be born with the virus. As of now, AIDS is nearly always fatal (deadly) and has no known cure.

5 Teen Parents and Their Futures

ALAN WAS REALLY WORRIED WHEN HIS
girlfriend, Melissa, got pregnant. They hadn't planned
on it. He liked her a lot, but he wasn't ready to marry
her, and he didn't want to be a father yet. He had big
plans to be a doctor. He was working hard in high
school to get into a good college with a strong medical
program.

Alan told Melissa that he would use his savings to
help her pay for an abortion. He was really surprised
when she said that she didn't want an abortion; she
wanted to keep the baby. "I don't expect you to marry
me, Alan," she said, much to his relief. "I'm prepared to
deal with this on my own. But I know I'll need help
with money. My parents aren't very supportive about
my keeping the baby."

Alan's savings went toward Melissa's doctor visits
and the hospital costs when the baby was born. After
that, he had no savings left. Then there were the day-to-
day expenses: money for diapers, food, clothes. He
had to take a part-time job to help Melissa pay for

everything. Then, when Melissa was ready to go back to school, there was the cost of day care too.

Alan had to start working more hours at his job. This gave him less time for studying. He was finding it hard to keep up—especially in the math and science courses that were so important for his med school plans. "I don't know what to do," Alan told his school counselor one day. "At this rate, I feel like I'll never be able to pay enough attention to my homework to get good grades. I'm really worried that I won't get a scholarship to college. All my savings for school have gone to the baby. Melissa and I aren't even together anymore, so it's like I'm taking care of a family I'm not even part of!"

Having a baby changes your life forever. We also know that having a child while you're still a teen means you have to face some pretty tough situations. Suddenly you are responsible for another human being that you have to love and provide for. We have seen that it is very expensive to raise a child. But what about the costs that aren't so easy to measure? What about hopes and dreams of a successful future? Does having a baby mean that you have to put aside all your dreams?

We've already seen how becoming a parent while you're still a teen can affect your life. In this chapter, we'll look at the impact of teen parenthood on educational and career goals. Since the

Having a baby as a teenager can make it difficult to accomplish goals such as a college education.

majority of teen parents are unmarried mothers raising their babies in single-parent homes, we'll also look at what kind of effect this can have on a child's future.

Teen Parents and School

The stereotype about teen parents, especially teen mothers, is that once they have a baby, they usually become high school dropouts with very little hope for the future. How accurate is this image? It is not completely false, but not completely true either. Let's look at the facts.

More teenage mothers are completing high school than ever before. A law passed in 1972 forbids discrimination against pregnant and parenting teens. Because of this law, there are many programs inside and outside of public high schools that make it easier for teen parents to stay in school. Such programs seem to work. Statistics tell us that women who attend special schools for pregnant and parenting teens do much better later in life than those who go to a regular high school or drop out.

However, compared to teens who are not parents, teen mothers finish high school at a lower rate, and those who do get their diplomas take much longer to finish their high school educations. About 70 percent of women who give birth as teenagers have finished high school by the time they are in their thirties, compared with 90 percent of older mothers. Teen mothers are much less likely to go on to college than their peers who wait until they are older than twenty years old to have children.

While all of this makes it look like having a baby as a teen *causes* a young woman to face more difficulties in finishing her education, it isn't necessarily so. Studies have been done that show that many teen parents were not doing well in school even before they became pregnant. Some were already high school dropouts.

Most teen moms who remain in school after their babies are born eventually graduate from high school. By comparison, only about 30 percent of women who drop out of high school before or after their babies are born eventually graduate. With this in mind, it seems truer to say that dropping out of school—not having a baby—is what makes teen parents have a tougher time than their peers later in life.

We've already learned that many teen mothers end up having a second child just a few years after their first. This can be a big obstacle to finishing high school. Imagine how difficult it would be to go to school every day and take care of two babies! Women who have two babies in their teens have a much harder time finishing school and getting a good job afterward.

Teenage fathers also face more obstacles than teens who are not fathers. They are much more likely to drop out of school—only 39 percent of teen fathers finish high school by the age of twenty, compared with 86 percent of male teens who aren't fathers. Also, teen fathers are less likely to finish college.

Most Poor Teens Remain Poor

The majority of teen mothers are from low-income backgrounds. They are also more likely than women who do not give birth before the age of twenty to be poor later on in their lives. In fact, about 28 percent of women who became moms when they were teens are poor in their twenties and early thirties, compared to 7 percent of women who did not give birth in their teens. One study found that teen mothers earn about half the lifetime income of women who first gave birth in their twenties.

Are teen moms poor later on in life *because* they were teen moms? This is a tricky question and not easy to answer. Research tells us that a substantial percentage of poor women who were teen mothers would have been poor anyway, even if they hadn't had babies when they were young. But there are still many who could have done better for themselves if they had waited until they were older to have a baby.

Are Married Teen Mothers Better Off?

Wendy's father left her family when she was five years old. After that, Wendy's mother raised Wendy and her brothers as a single mom. Working two jobs, her mom had hardly any time to spend with the kids. It bothered Wendy that her mom was never home and that even as hard as her mom worked, there never seemed to be enough money.

So when Wendy's boyfriend, Rashid, suggested that they get married, Wendy was excited. Here was her chance to move out and run her own household the way she wanted. She vowed that she would spend lots of time with her own kids and that she and Rashid would always give the kids anything they wanted. "It'll be easier for me than it was for my mom, because Rashid will be around," Wendy thought.

Rashid and Wendy got married soon after they both turned eighteen. Within a few months, Wendy got pregnant. The timing wasn't very good, since Wendy was scheduled to start at the community college the month the baby was due. So she withdrew from the college, thinking that she would start after the baby was born. But the baby took a lot of time, and she and Rashid couldn't afford day care, so she continued to stay at home. Rashid, meanwhile, was the only one earning

Married teens with children have a tough time getting by just as unmarried teen parents do.

money, so he had to take another job to support Wendy and the baby. He wasn't home very much.

Spending her days taking care of her baby alone, Wendy started to wonder about her decision to get married and start a family so young. She almost never saw Rashid, and she worried that unless she got more education, she wouldn't be able to give her child the life she had planned. Talking to her friend Jenny on the phone one day, Wendy said, "You know, I never wanted to be a single mom and go through the tough times like my mom did. But being married with a kid is pretty tough too."

The overwhelming majority of teen mothers are not married when they have their babies. What does this mean for the mother and for the future of her baby? There are many people who believe that children who grow up in single-parent homes do much worse in life than children whose parents are married and live together. Other people believe that it doesn't matter how many parents raise the child, as long as he or she feels loved and wanted.

Like most of the tough issues we've already looked at, there is both truth and fiction behind the stereotypes about single-parent homes.

Research has shown that children who grow up with only one parent in the home (almost always the mother) are more disadvantaged in a variety of ways than children who are raised by both parents. They are more likely to drop out of school, become teen parents themselves, and have trouble finding jobs when they grow up. But problems exist in two-parent families as well.

Girls who marry their baby's father after they become pregnant are less likely to go back to school after their baby is born. One reason for this might be that if a teen girl marries and moves in with her husband, away from her home, she has less help in taking care of her child, since so many teen mothers get help from their own mothers. One study of adolescent mothers found that those who remained at their parents' home in the first five years after the child's birth were more likely to graduate from high school, find work, and not be dependent on welfare.

Some believe that if a teen marries, she will be more financially secure and less likely to be on welfare. Indeed 75 percent of unmarried teens go on welfare within five years of childbirth. However, marriage is no guarantee against welfare. Twenty-five percent of girls who were married when they gave birth go on welfare within five years.

Loretta didn't plan on having a baby at sixteen, but when she and her boyfriend, Eric, learned that she was pregnant, they decided to get married and raise the

Few young men are able to earn enough money to support a family, especially if they have only a high school education.

baby as best they could. Loretta is a high school senior, with plans to go to college to study computer programming. She knows that trying to fulfill her goals will be more difficult with a baby taking so much of her time, but she's heard of other girls who've made it work. Eric finished high school last year and just started to attend a local college. He decided to stop going to college for awhile and is looking for a full-time job to support the family. But without a college degree, he's having a hard time finding a well-paying job.

A young father with the best intentions to support his family still faces many obstacles. Less than half of young men in their early twenties earn enough money to support a family of three.

Even if a girl does not marry her baby's father, she and her child are still entitled to receive money from him to help pay for child care. This is called child support. A big problem faced by single mothers is the fact that very often, the fathers of their children do not pay child support like they are supposed to. Child support can be very hard to collect, especially if the father is out of work, or moves away to another city or state. Not paying child support is a crime.

6 Staying on the Right Track

WHAT CAN YOU DO TO MAKE SURE YOU DON'T become a parent before you are ready for the responsibility? Preventing pregnancy is the first step. Anytime you have sex, you or your partner can get pregnant—even if it is the first time you have sex and even if you are using birth control. The only way you can guarantee that you will not get pregnant is by practicing abstinence—not having sex at all.

If you do decide to have sex, it is very important to use birth control. Make sure that you always use a condom and, ideally, an additional form of birth control. Condoms protect against sexually transmitted diseases, including AIDS, and should be used every time you have sex. Speak with your doctor or with a counselor at a clinic about another form of birth control to use with the condom, such as the Pill, diaphragm, and cervical cap. You can purchase spermicidal jellies and foams

Teachers and counselors can help you to develop goals and priorities.

in a drugstore. The female condom is another option.

Remember that any birth control method can fail, especially if it is not used correctly. Most teenagers who become parents do not plan to get pregnant—either they did not use birth control, or the method they used did not work.

If your parents haven't talked to you about sex, and you have questions you want to ask, don't be afraid to speak up. There's nothing wrong with talking about sex and pregnancy prevention. Your parents may be very relieved that you came to them for guidance. If you can't talk to your parents, talk to another adult you trust. This might be a family friend, an aunt or uncle, a favorite teacher, or a school counselor.

In addition to protecting against pregnancy, it is also important to set goals for yourself and work toward them. You have read in this book about how some teens become parents because they lack confidence in their futures. Think about where you want to be five or ten years from now. What do you need to do to get there? If you want to be an auto mechanic, maybe you can get a part-time job at an auto shop. If you plan to be a teacher, ask your favorite teacher at school if you might be able to help him or her before or after school. Talk to your parents, a teacher, or a counselor about your thoughts on the future. They will probably have ideas about how you can explore different careers.

If one of your lifelong dreams is to be a parent, that's fine too, but there's no need to hurry. You have many years in which to become a parent, and in the meantime you can focus on yourself. Getting a good education and a good career will pay off in the long run and will make parenthood more rewarding. You will be able to feel good about providing a good life for your children. And you will feel good about yourself because you will know that you gave yourself the time to achieve your own goals. Going back to school or getting the training for the career of your dreams will be harder to do

Many women today are choosing to focus on their career goals before starting families. Staying in school can help you get the education and skills you will need for a successful career.

when you have to think about providing for a child's everyday needs.

The world of work is becoming more competitive, demanding that workers have more education and training than ever before. The system of welfare is no longer the same; families will no longer be guaranteed a check every month. This situation is scary, but there is still plenty of opportunity for people who are willing to work for their goals. Waiting to have children is a way to give yourself an even better chance of success.

Glossary

abortion Ending a pregnancy by removing the fetus (the unborn baby in its very early stages) from the womb before it can survive outside the womb.

abstinence Complete avoidance of a particular activity, such as sex.

AFDC **(Aid to Families with Dependent Children)** The largest program of the federal welfare system. The program ended in 1996.

AIDS **(Acquired Immunodeficiency Syndrome)** A disease, which is almost always fatal, caused by the Human Immunodeficiency Virus (HIV).

anemia A low red blood cell count.

birth control Methods used to prevent pregnancy.

child support Money paid by a child's father when he is not part of the household.

contraceptive Any device used to prevent pregnancy.

first trimester The first three months of pregnancy.

HIV **(Human Immunodeficiency Virus)** A virus transmitted through bodily fluids, such as blood and semen.

premarital sex Sex before marriage.

premature birth The birth of a baby before it has fully developed and is physically ready to leave the womb.

prenatal care Medical care of a mother and baby before the baby is born.

sexually transmitted disease (STD) Any disease that is spread through sexual activity, such as AIDS, gonorrhea, herpes, syphilis, and chlamydia.

Help List

Advocates for Youth
1025 Vermont Avenue, NW, Suite 200
Washington, DC 20005
(202) 347-5700
e-mail: info@advocatesforyouth.org

Big Brothers Big Sisters of America
230 North 13th Street
Philadelphia, PA 19107
(215) 567-7000
e-mail: bbbsa@aol.com
Web site: http://www.bbbsa.org

Planned Parenthood Federation of America
810 Seventh Avenue
New York, NY 10019
(212) 541-7800
e-mail: communications@ppfa.org
Web site: http://www.ppfa.org/ppfa/

Pregnancy Crisis Center Hot Line
(800) 492-5530

Sexually Transmitted Disease Hot Line
(800) 227-8922

In Canada:

Planned Parenthood Federation of Canada
1 Nicholas Street, Suite 430
Ottawa, Ontario K1N 7B7
(613) 241-4474

For Further Reading

Bode, Janet. *Kids Having Kids: People Talk About Teen Pregnancy.* New York: Franklin Watts, 1992.

Kuklin, Susan. *What Do I Do Now? Talking About Teenage Pregnancy.* New York: G. P. Putnam's Sons, 1991.

Pollock, Sudie. *Will the Dollars Stretch? Teen Parents Living on Their Own.* Buena Park, CA: Morning Glory Press, 1997.

Weiss, Ann E. *Welfare: Helping Hand or Trap?* Hillside, NJ: Enslow Publishers, 1990.

Westheimer, Ruth. *Dr. Ruth Talks to Kids.* New York: Macmillan Books for Young Readers, 1993.

Index

A
adolescence, 7
AFDC (Aid to Families with Dependent Children), 28–29, 30, 32–34, 36
AIDS (Acquired Immunodeficiency Syndrome), 10, 20, 40, 53

B
birth control, 10, 13–14, 20–21, 23, 31, 53–54
boyfriends, 20–21

C
Canada, 35
child care, 24, 25–27, 42, 50–52
child support, 24, 52
condoms, 8, 10, 20, 40, 53–54
cost of raising child, 25–26, 41

D
discrimination, 44

F
family support, 23–24, 28

H
HIV (Human Immunodeficiency Virus), 20, 40
households
divorced parents, 22
single-parent, 22, 26, 44, 49–50
two-parent, 8, 34, 49, 50

I
income, 10–11, 16, 46–47

M
marriage, 22–23, 30, 34–35, 41, 47–52
media influences, 23
Medicaid, 11, 36

P
peer pressure, 18, 20
Pill, the, 10, 20, 53
pregnancy
discussing with parents, 14–15
hiding, 13–14
pregnancy choices, 12–13
abortion, 8, 11–13, 41
adoption, 8, 26

About the Author
Barbara Miller is a cultural anthropologist specializing in education and documentary film. She has conducted extensive research on various issues related to teens.

Photo Credits
Cover by Ira Fox; p. 15 by Maria Moreno; p. 22 by Guillermina DeFerrari; p. 51 by Yung-Hee Chia. All other photos by Ira Fox.

Layout and Design
Erin McKenna